The Story of Our Holidays

THANKSGIVING

Joanna Ponto

Enslow Publishing
101 W. 23rd Street
Suite 240
New York, NY 10011
USA

enslow.com

Published in 2017 by Enslow Publishing, LLC.
101 W. 23rd Street, Suite 240, New York, NY 10011

Library of Congress Cataloging-in-Publication Data
Names: Ponto, Joanna, author.
Title: Thanksgiving / Joanna Ponto.
Description: New York, NY : Enslow Publishing, [2017] | Series: The story of our holidays | Includes bibliographical references and index.
Identifiers: LCCN 2016001038| ISBN 9780766076341 (library bound) | ISBN 9780766076310 (pbk.) | ISBN 9780766076334 (6-pack)
Subjects: LCSH: Thanksgiving Day--Juvenile literature.
Classification: LCC GT4975 .P65 2016 | DDC 394.2649--dc23
LC record available at http://lccn.loc.gov/2016001038

Printed in the United States of America

To Our Readers: We have done our best to make sure all website addresses in this book were active and appropriate when we went to press. However, the author and the publisher have no control over and assume no liability for the material available on those websites or on any websites they may link to. Any comments or suggestions can be sent by e-mail to customerservice@enslow.com.

Portions of this book originally appeared in the book *Thanksgiving Day: A Time to Be Thankful* by Elaine Landau.

Photos Credits: Cover, p. 1 Brian Leatart/Photolibrary/Getty Images; p. 4 Monkey Business Images/Shutterstock.com; p. 7 Brent Hofacker/Shutterstock.com; p. 8 Voraorn Ratanakorn/Shutterstock.com; p. 9 Tova Teitelbaum/Getty Images; p. 11 American School/Getty Images; p. 13 Bridgeman Images; p. 15 Everett Historical/Shutterstock.com; p. 17 Library of Congress; p. 19 Jim Cole/AP Images; p. 20 Margaret Bourke-White/Getty Images; p. 22 A. Katz/Shutterstock.com; p. 24 The Sacramento Bee/AP Images; p. 25 John Bazemore/AP Images; p. 27 Stephen Jaffe/AFP/Getty Images; p. 29 © Karen Huang.

Crafts made by Sophie Hayn and Aniya Strickland.

Contents

Every year, Americans come together to celebrate Thanksgiving.

Chapter 1

Give Thanks

Many of our favorite holidays involve food and other treats that we look forward to all year. But there is a certain dinner that we associate with one holiday in particular. Turkey . . . stuffing . . . cranberries . . . pumpkin pie. These foods probably do not make you think of St. Patrick's Day or Valentine's Day. These are Thanksgiving treats.

A Special Meal

Americans celebrate Thanksgiving every year on the last Thursday of November. It is a special day for many reasons. Friends and family come together. Some people travel many miles to be together. They enjoy good food and good times.

On Thanksgiving Day everyone looks forward to the meal. In most homes it is a busy time for the cook. Many Americans eat turkey on that day. About 45 million pounds (22.5 million kilograms) of turkey are eaten every Thanksgiving. With it, we have 65 million pounds (32.5 million kg) of sweet potatoes and 80 million pounds of cranberries (40 million kg). Try making cranberry sauce using the recipe on the next page. For dessert, 55 million pumpkin pies are served.

Harvest Celebrations

Thanksgiving has been celebrated in America for more than three hundred fifty years. It began as a harvest festival. After a hard winter, the early settlers, known as Pilgrims, had a good harvest of many crops. They celebrated with a feast. That is why we think of Thanksgiving as an American holiday.

People around the world have always celebrated good harvests. Some of these celebrations date back to long ago. The names and dates may be different, but the idea behind them is the same.

Ancient Romans had a harvest feast, known as Cerelia, in early October. This is where the word cereal comes from. They thanked Ceres, the corn goddess. There was also music, parades, and games.

Chinese people celebrated good harvests, too. Thousands of years ago they held a three-day Moon Festival. Roast pig and harvest fruits

Thanksgiving Cranberry Sauce*

Ingredients:

1 12-oz bag fresh cranberries
1 pear, peeled, cored, and diced
1 cup sugar
1 stick cinnamon
Juice and zest of one orange
½ oz fresh ginger, sliced
½ cup of water

Directions:

1. In a medium saucepan over medium-high heat, add all ingredients and cover.

2. Once boiling, reduce heat to simmer. Stir gently to make sure all ingredients are well mixed. Be sure not to use a wooden spoon… it will get stained!

3. Keep an eye on the pot. As the water boils, the cranberries will pop. The liquid will get thicker, and everything will become a rich red color.

4. Stir the sauce to ensure that all the cranberries have popped. If they haven't, just use your spoon and squish the berries against the side of the pot.

5. Before serving, take out the pieces of ginger and the cinnamon stick.

6. Enjoy with turkey or ham, dressing, or over vanilla ice cream as a day-after-Thanksgiving dessert!

7   * Adult supervision required.

Moon cakes are enjoyed by Chinese people during the Moon, or Mid-Autumn, festival.

were served. There were small round cakes and yellow candies that looked like the full moon.

Jewish people also have a harvest festival called Sukkoth. Sukkoth began more than three thousand years ago. It is still celebrated every autumn. Some families build a small hut made of tree branches for the festival. Leaves are spread over its roof. Apples, grapes, corn, and other vegetables are hung inside. The festival is eight days. The first

Coming Together

Each year, on the last Thursday in the month of November, people all over the United States celebrate Thanksgiving. It is a special time for families and friends to come together and give thanks.

two nights are special. On those nights, families eat dinner in the hut. American Jews may celebrate both Sukkoth and Thanksgiving.

An American Holiday

Thanksgiving is a time for all Americans to feast and give thanks. Many families begin their Thanksgiving meal with a prayer. Others attend a religious service. They think about all the things for which they are grateful.

People start preparing for Thanksgiving weeks ahead of time. Some use old family recipes. Often favorite dishes are served. On Thanksgiving, many people eat more than usual. It is okay to have some extra stuffing or a second slice of pie. It is almost expected. But Thanksgiving is much more than an extra slice of pie. It is about appreciating American life.

Most Americans associate Thanksgiving with a big meal.

Chapter 2

Thanksgiving's Origins

Thanksgiving is an American tradition that began hundreds of years ago. The holiday marks a special feast that took place when the American colonies were first being settled.

The Pilgrims' Land

Thanksgiving began in Plymouth, Massachusetts, in 1620. A group of people known as Pilgrims had just arrived from England. The Pilgrims hoped to lead a life devoted to God in a new land. But first, they had to build a place to live, and that would not be easy.

Their trip from England was also not easy. On September 16, 1620, the Pilgrims set sail on a small ship named the *Mayflower*.

The voyage was long and cold. There were rough storms at sea. The passengers were often seasick. One man died.

Their first months in America were even worse than the voyage. The Pilgrims arrived in December. It was a very cold winter, and they did not have enough food. Many Pilgrims became ill, and some of them died. One hundred two people had sailed on the *Mayflower*. By spring, just fifty-seven of them were alive.

The Pilgrims refused to give up. They tried to plant crops from seeds they had brought from England. But the seeds would not grow in the rocky soil.

These settlers were also not used to catching or hunting for their food. They did not know how to track a deer or where to find the best fish. But then help came.

When the Pilgrims arrived in the New World, they had no idea how difficult it would be to survive. Most had no idea how to hunt or grow crops.

Help from Indians

The Pilgrims had seen American Indians near their village, but the Pilgrims had not spoken to them. That changed on Friday, March 16, 1621. An American Indian named Samoset came to their village. He greeted them saying, "Welcome, Englishmen." The Pilgrims were very surprised to learn that Samoset spoke English. He had learned the language from English fishermen who came to America each year to fish.

Samoset spoke with the Pilgrims. He knew the area well. There had been an Indian village there, but it had been wiped out by disease. Samoset returned a few days later. This time, he brought a friend named Squanto. Like Samoset, Squanto also spoke English.

Squanto helped the Pilgrims. He stayed with them for several months. Their new Indian friend knew which crops would grow. Squanto gave the Pilgrims seeds for corn, squash, and pumpkins. Other vegetables were planted, too. He taught them to bury a dead fish wherever they planted seeds. This fed the soil and helped the plants grow.

Squanto took the Pilgrims into the forest. The men learned to hunt for deer, rabbits, and wild turkey. Squanto also taught them to make good use of the waters in the area. Before long, the Pilgrims were

Squanto showed the Pilgrims how to plant crops. He buried dead fish in the soil as fertilizer. This helped the crops grow.

trapping lobsters and digging for clams.

The women and children gathered wild fruits and berries. They learned which were good to eat and which were poisonous. The Indians had used herbs and plants as medicines for a long time. Now, the Pilgrims used them, too.

A Harvest Feast

The Pilgrims might not have survived that first year without Squanto's help. But with it they succeeded. By fall 1621 the Pilgrims had a rich harvest. There was enough food for the coming winter. They decided to celebrate with a feast.

William Bradford was the Pilgrims' governor. He invited Squanto to the feast. Governor Bradford also told Squanto to bring some friends. To the Pilgrims' surprise, ninety Indians showed up. They did not come empty-handed, though. The Indians brought five deer, so there was plenty of food for everyone.

The foods they ate that day are not what many of us eat at Thanksgiving today. There was venison (deer) that the Indians brought and wild turkey. The Pilgrims hunted rabbits, ducks, and geese, which were probably also served. Eel, codfish, sea bass, and clams were probably other foods at the feast.

There was no pumpkin pie. The Pilgrims' supply of flour had run out. While they had no cakes or cookies of any kind, they did eat boiled pumpkin, wild fruits, and berries.

No one knows the exact days when the feast took place, but it was probably sometime in mid-

Samoset and Squanto

The American Indians helped the Pilgrims by showing them how to plant crops and hunt for deer and rabbits. The Pilgrims owed a great debt to the American Indian chief known as Samoset and another Indian named Squanto.

To celebrate the harvest, the Pilgrims hosted a feast. They invited the Indians, who were partly responsible for their success.

October. The feast lasted three days. The women cooked the food over outdoor fires. Everyone ate outside at long tables. The Pilgrims and the Indians played games. There were footraces, too. The Pilgrims showed off their skills with a musket, a type of gun. The Indians did the same with a bow and arrow.

The Pilgrims enjoyed the feast. But they did not think of it as a time for giving thanks. To them, giving thanks meant hours of prayer and fasting instead of eating.

The harvest feast was not held every year. Some years crops failed and there was little reason to celebrate. Yet people liked the idea of Pilgrims and Indians sharing a feast. Over time, this harvest feast came to be known as the first Thanksgiving.

Chapter 3

A Reluctant Holiday

The first Thanksgiving did not catch on as a holiday. Other New England colonies heard about the Pilgrims' harvest feast. Some had their own Thanksgiving celebrations. But those feasts did not take place every year, and no special dates were set.

The Holiday Slowly Spreads

During the American Revolution, when the American colonies fought for freedom from English rule, several days were set aside for giving thanks. These days were usually after important victories. The first Thanksgiving Day for the entire country, however, was not until November 26, 1789. President George Washington ordered it, but the custom did not catch on.

George Washington requested a day to celebrate "humble thanks" for the "protection of the People of this Country previous to their becoming a Nation."

A Long Time Coming

President George Washington ordered that the first Thanksgiving Day for the entire country should be held on November 26, 1789. But the holiday did not turn into Thanksgiving as we know it until much later.

In time, some states started their own Thanksgiving Day. New York was one of the first states to do so. By 1817, Thanksgiving was celebrated every year in New York. Other northern states did the same thing. Virginia was the first southern state to follow their lead. Thanksgiving Day became a state holiday there in 1855. The holiday was usually celebrated in November, but different states held it on different days.

The Mother of Thanksgiving

People seemed not to see the need for a national Thanksgiving Day. But one woman did not feel this way. Her name was Sarah Josepha Hale. She is sometimes known as the "mother" of Thanksgiving.

Hale was a magazine editor. Every fall she filled her magazine with Thanksgiving stories, songs, and recipes.

Hale thought that Thanksgiving should be celebrated throughout the United States. So she began writing letters to governors and presidents. Support for her idea began to grow.

A Federal Holiday

After many years Hale's work paid off. In 1863, President Abraham Lincoln declared a day of Thanksgiving for the whole country. It was set on the last Thursday of November. Every president after Lincoln did the same. This custom continued for seventy-five years.

In 1939, President Franklin D. Roosevelt changed the holiday to the third Thursday of November. This was a week earlier than usual. The president wanted to help American businesses. He hoped making the holiday earlier would

Sarah Josepha Hale lobbied for Thanksgiving to be recognized as a national holiday.

President Franklin Delano Roosevelt carves the Thanksgiving turkey alongside his wife, First Lady Eleanor Roosevelt, in 1938.

make the Christmas shopping season last longer.

But the public did not like the idea of moving the holiday. People were not sure when to celebrate Thanksgiving Day. Some tried the new date. Others celebrated when they always had. Still others celebrated on both days.

Congress finally set things straight in 1941. Thanksgiving Day was declared a federal holiday. This means the United States government said it was an official holiday. The date was changed back to the last Thursday in November. On that day all government offices are closed. So are schools, banks, and most businesses. There is no mail delivery. In homes throughout the nation, people celebrate the day and give thanks.

Chapter 4

Celebrating Thanksgiving

The first Thanksgiving celebrated the harvest. Today, we continue the tradition by enjoying a huge meal. But Americans do more than eat on this holiday.

I Love a Parade

Many enjoy watching Thanksgiving Day parades. Some of the larger parades are in New York City, Detroit, Houston, and Philadelphia. The best-known parade is in New York City. It is Macy's annual Thanksgiving Day Parade. Millions of Americans watch it on television each year.

The parade has marching bands and clowns. There are also huge balloons filled with helium, a gas that is lighter than air. It allows the giant balloons to float high above the crowds. The balloons are shaped like well-known cartoon and storybook characters. Favorites include Snoopy and Felix the cat.

For some people who live nearby, there is a special treat. The fun starts the night before the parade. They can watch the Thanksgiving Day balloons being filled with helium. It is exciting to see the different characters take shape.

Fun and Games

The Pilgrims and American Indians ran races at their Thanksgiving feast. There were games, too. Sports are still an important part of

Thanksgiving Day. Football games are especially popular. High school teams play against one another.

Macy's sponsors the famous Thanksgiving Day Parade in New York City.

Some families like playing touch football in their yards.

Americans also watch football on television on Thanksgiving Day. Two National Football League (NFL) teams host holiday games. They are the Detroit Lions and the Dallas Cowboys. Many people eagerly look forward to these games. They have become part of an American Thanksgiving.

But not everyone watches or plays football on Thanksgiving. Footraces are fun, too. That is how many Texans in Dallas begin the holiday. They take part in the YMCA's Turkey Trot. More than twenty thousand people run in the race. Then they head home for Thanksgiving dinner.

The Run for Diamonds is held every Thanksgiving, as well. It is a nine-mile race in Berwick, Pennsylvania. There are many wonderful prizes. The top seven male runners get diamond rings. The top seven female runners get diamond pendants. Other races are held in many

The Macy's Parade

Macy's Thanksgiving Day Parade features other spectacles besides its giant balloons. Singers, dancers, and marching bands all march or ride on floats down the parade route to entertain the crowds. There is even a visit from Santa Claus at the end of the parade!

Turkey trots and other races are popular on Thanksgiving Day. Some people enjoy burning calories before they sit down to a big Thanksgiving meal!

towns and cities. The prizes vary. Sometimes winners get dessert. They can take home a pumpkin or a pecan pie.

One Thanksgiving Day race held in Minneapolis, Minnesota, has a special twist. The Northwest Athletic Club's run helps the whole community. Runners enjoy the holiday race, but something more important also goes on. Throughout the whole month of November, club members bring food to ten places throughout the city. On Thanksgiving morning, the food is loaded onto trucks and taken to a food bank. A food bank is a place where food is collected and stored. From there, it is given out to people who need it.

Helping Others

Others have also tried to make a difference on Thanksgiving. In Harrisburg, Pennsylvania, community groups work together to give turkeys to hundreds of needy families. Similar projects take place in other areas.

Soup kitchens feed the homeless and hungry all year, but they are especially busy on Thanksgiving Day. Many host special holiday dinners. Usually volunteers spend the day helping. They cook and serve the food and clean up afterward. Often the volunteers are students. They help give others a reason to be thankful and experience the true meaning of this holiday.

Many give back to those in need on Thanksgiving. They may volunteer at a soup kitchen or deliver meals to people who cannot leave their homes.

Everyone deserves a wonderful Thanksgiving. But the holiday is never much fun for turkeys. That is why every Thanksgiving Eve the president of the United States pardons one very lucky turkey. This fortunate bird never reaches a dinner table. Instead, it goes to a Virginia petting farm. It remains there for the rest of its life. This custom began more than fifty years ago. President Harry Truman started it. The presidents who came after him have continued to follow this custom.

Thanksgiving Travel

Just as the turkey that is saved leaves town, many people also go away for Thanksgiving. Some people visit family and friends, and others go to different places. On the day before Thanksgiving, airports and highways are often crowded. It is the busiest travel day of the year.

There are many interesting Thanksgiving vacation spots. One is the Ozark Folk Center in Mountainview, Arkansas. There, you can see how mountain people once lived. It is fun to watch a blacksmith work or learn how cider is made from apples. On Thanksgiving Day a special meal is served. Then there is a Thanksgiving Gospel Concert.

Part of the official duties of the president of the United States is letting one turkey off the hook every Thanksgiving. Bill Clinton gave the nod to this turkey in 1999. However, most turkeys aren't so lucky!

Another great Thanksgiving stop is Plimoth Plantation near Plymouth, Massachusetts. The plantation looks just like the Pilgrims' village. Actors dress and act as the early settlers and Indians did.

It is good to step back into history. We can learn how Thanksgiving Day was once celebrated. But trying new things is important, too. Thanksgiving Day is about being grateful. It is also about caring. Challenge yourself this Thanksgiving. See how many ways you can show these feelings. You will be creating your own Thanksgiving traditions.

Thanksgiving Craft*

After you help set the dinner table, set the holiday mood with these seating cards to tell everyone where to sit.

Here are the supplies you will need:

brown wrapping paper or a brown paper bag cut open
a pencil
red, orange, and yellow crayons or markers
safety scissors

Directions:

1. Place your hand on the paper.

2. Spread your fingers apart.

3. Trace the outline of your hand and fingers. Your palm is the turkey's body. Your fingers are its feathers. Your thumb is its head.

4. Color the feathers red, orange, and yellow.

5. Write a person's name on the turkey's body.

6. Cut out the outline.

7. Be sure to make one for each person at dinner. Place a turkey seating card on the table in front of each seat.

Turkey Seating Cards

*Safety note: Be sure to ask for help from an adult, if needed, to complete this project.

Glossary

custom—The way a group of people does something.

editor—A person who corrects written work for a magazine or a book.

fasting—Going without food.

harvest—To gather crops.

origin—The beginning of something, or when something is created.

pendant—A charm or locket to put on a necklace.

Pilgrims—A group of English settlers who founded the colony of Plymouth, Massachusetts, in 1620.

reluctant—Not wanting to do something.

tradition—To do something the same way each time it is done.

venison—The meat of a deer.

Learn More

Books

Dash, Meredith. *Thanksgiving.* Minneapolis, MN: ABDO Kids, 2014.

Herrington, Lisa. *Thanksgiving.* New York, NY: Children's Press, 2014.

Keogh, Josie. *Thanksgiving.* New York, NY: PowerKids Press, 2013.

Pettiford, Rebecca. *Thanksgiving.* Minneapolis, MN: Jump! Inc., 2016.

Websites

Enchanted Learning Thanksgiving Crafts

enchantedlearning.com/crafts/thanksgiving
With crafts, worksheets, and printable books all relating to Thanksgiving, you'll have plenty to keep yourself busy!

Family Education Thanksgiving page

fun.familyeducation.com/thanksgiving/activities/33069.html
This resource features Thanksgiving crafts, recipes, puzzles, and questions you can ask your family at the dinner table.

Pilgrim Hall Museum

pilgrimhall.org/thanksg.htm
This museum teaches about the Pilgrims' experience with artifacts from their colony.

Index